SandCastle

United We Stand

Tolerance

Pam Scheunemann

Consulting Editor
Monica Marx, M.A./Reading Specialist

ABDO
Publishing Company

Published by SandCastle™, an imprint of ABDO Publishing Company, 4940 Viking Drive, Edina, Minnesota 55435.

Printed in the United States.

Credits
Edited by: Pam Price
Curriculum Coordinator: Nancy Tuminelly
Cover and Interior Design and Production: Mighty Media
Photo Credits: Corbis Images, Eyewire Images, PhotoDisc, Skjold Photography

Library of Congress Cataloging-in-Publication Data
Scheunemann, Pam, 1955-
    Tolerance / Pam Scheunemann.
        p. cm. -- (United we stand)
    Includes index.
    Summary: Discusses the nature of tolerance, which means accepting people no matter what they look like, how they live, what they like, or how they do things.
    ISBN 1-57765-881-7
    1. Toleration--Juvenile literature. [1. Toleration. 2. Prejudices.] I. Title. II. Series.

HM1271 .S38 2002
302'.14--dc21
                                                                                    2002066400

SandCastle™ books are created by a professional team of educators, reading specialists, and content developers around five essential components that include phonemic awareness, phonics, vocabulary, text comprehension, and fluency. All books are written, reviewed, and leveled for guided reading, early intervention reading, and Accelerated Reader® programs and designed for use in shared, guided, and independent reading and writing activities to support a balanced approach to literacy instruction.

Let Us Know

After reading the book, SandCastle would like you to tell us your stories about reading. What is your favorite page? Was there something hard that you needed help with? Share the ups and downs of learning to read. We want to hear from you! To get posted on the ABDO Publishing Company Web site, send us email at:

sandcastle@abdopub.com

SandCastle Level: Transitional

What is tolerance?

Tolerance means accepting people for who they are.

People look different.

Tolerance means accepting people no matter what they look like.

Mari, Kim, Jon, and Ali are smiling.

People have different ways of life.

Tolerance means accepting people no matter how they live.

Sue wears special holiday clothes.

People like to do different things.

Tolerance means accepting people no matter what they like to do.

Maya and Ellen like basketball.

People do things differently.

Tolerance means accepting people no matter how they do things.

Kris likes to look closely at things.

Some people have blue eyes and some people have brown eyes.

But we all have eyes.

Liz and Rita are having fun.

Some people live in apartments and some people live in houses.

But we all have a place we call home.

Some homes are in the city.

Some people like hamburgers and some people like hot dogs.

But we all have a favorite food.

Bob and his dad like hamburgers.

Some people are good at art and some people are good at math.

What are you good at?

Index

Glossary

accept to agree with something

apartment a set of rooms to live in that is in a building with other apartments

different things or people that are not alike

favorite someone or something that you like best

some an unknown number of people or things

tolerance to be accepting of people different from ourselves

About SandCastle™

A professional team of educators, reading specialists, and content developers created the SandCastle™ series to support young readers as they develop reading skills and strategies and increase their general knowledge. The SandCastle™ series has four levels that correspond to early literacy development in young children. The levels are provided to help teachers and parents select the appropriate books for young readers.

Emerging Readers
(no flags)

Beginning Readers
(1 flag)

Transitional Readers
(2 flags)

Fluent Readers
(3 flags)

These levels are meant only as a guide. All levels are subject to change.

ABDO
Publishing Company

To see a complete list of SandCastle™ books and other nonfiction titles from ABDO Publishing Company, visit www.abdopub.com or contact us at:

4940 Viking Drive, Edina, Minnesota 55435 • 1-800-800-1312 • fax: 1-952-831-1632